I0605090

FROM THE PUBLISHER

Christina Rossetti's work cannot be fully appreciated without some knowledge of her history and her place among the arts. As the youngest of four children in a Victorian London family that valued both painting and writing, Christina's creative journey was surprisingly one of isolation and reflection. Her early works were of classical form, and relied on the Bible, religious writings, and folktales for inspiration. One of her brothers, painter Dante Gabriel Rossetti, became a very influential artist and poet as well as a founding member of the Pre-Raphaelite Brotherhood. That artistic influence also affected Christina's writing, infusing it with the traditions and subjects that the Pre-Raphaelites embraced.

With a strong religious bearing and her family's appreciation for poetry and literature all around her, her works often explored meditations, devotion, and the mysteries of death. Rossetti became the most important female poet of her time. *Goblin Market and Other Poems* (1862) would be her most famous collection—the title piece combining fairy-tale fantasy with themes of temptation, salvation, and redemption.

Illustrator Florence Harrison would likely have known and been influenced by Rossetti's works as a child. In 1910, when Scottish publisher Blackie & Son, Ltd. collected Rossetti's works into a large volume, they had already been working with Harrison for five years. Her own Pre-Raphaelite leanings paired her ethereal imagery well with Rossetti's poetry. Harrison was so drawn to the material that she handed in more color work than was commissioned, creating a memorable volume as beautiful to look at as it is to read.

GOBLIN MARKET

and other selected poems

My heart is like a singing bird

A Birthday.

GOBLIN MARKET

and other selected poems

CHRISTINA ROSSETTI

CALLA EDITIONS
MINEOLA, NEW YORK

Bibliographical Note

This Calla edition, first published in 2018, is an unabridged republication, in one volume, of *Goblin Market and Other Poems* and *Shorter Poems,* both by Christina Rossetti and illustrated by Florence Harrison, and originally published by Blackie & Son, Ltd., London, c. 1910.

International Standard Book Number

ISBN-13: 978-1-60660-120-4
ISBN-10: 1-60660-120-2

Calla Editions
An Imprint of Dover Publications, Inc.
www.doverpublications.com/calla

Printed in China by RR Donnelley

Contents

MORNING and evening
Maids heard the goblins cry:
"Come buy our orchard fruits,
Come buy, come buy:
Apples and quinces,
Lemons and oranges,
Plump unpecked cherries,
Melons and raspberries,
Bloom-down-cheeked peaches,
Swart-headed mulberries,
Wild free-born cranberries,
Crab-apples, dewberries,
Pine-apples, blackberries,
Apricots, strawberries;—
All ripe together
In summer weather,—
Morns that pass by,
Fair eves that fly;
Come buy, come buy:

Our grapes fresh from the vine
Pomegranates full and fine,
Dates and sharp bullaces,
Rare pears and greengages,
Damsons and bilberries,
Taste them and try:
Currants and gooseberries,
Bright fire-like barberries,
Figs to fill your mouth,
Citrons from the South,
Sweet to tongue and sound to eye;
Come buy, come buy."

Evening by evening
Among the brookside rushes,
Laura bowed her head to hear,
Lizzie veiled her blushes:
Crouching close together
In the cooling weather,
With clasping arms and cautioning lips
With tingling cheeks and finger tips.
"Lie close," Laura said,
Pricking up her golden head:
"We must not look at goblin men,
We must not buy their fruits:
Who knows upon what soil they fed
Their hungry, thirsty roots?"
"Come buy," call the goblins
Hobbling down the glen.
"Oh," cried Lizzie, "Laura, Laura,
You should not peep at goblin men."
Lizzie covered up her eyes,
Covered close lest they should look;

Sucked their fruit globes fair or red

Goblin Market.

Laura reared her glossy head,
And whispered like the restless brook:
" Look, Lizzie, look, Lizzie,
Down the glen tramp little men.
One hauls a basket,
One bears a plate,
One lugs a golden dish
Of many pounds weight.
How fair the vine must grow
Whose grapes are so luscious;
How warm the wind must blow
Through those fruit bushes."
"No," said Lizzie: "No, no, no;
Their offers should not charm us,
Their evil gifts would harm us."
She thrust a dimpled finger
In each ear, shut eyes and ran:
Curious Laura chose to linger
Wondering at each merchant man.
One had a cat's face,
One whisked a tail,
One tramped at a rat's pace,
One crawled like a snail,
One like a wombat prowled obtuse and furry,
One like a ratel tumbled hurry skurry.
She heard a voice like voice of doves
Cooing all together:
They sounded kind and full of loves
In the pleasant weather.

Laura stretched her gleaming neck
Like a rush-imbedded swan,

Like a lily from the beck,
Like a moonlit poplar branch,
Like a vessel at the launch
When its last restraint is gone.

Backwards up the mossy glen
Turned and trooped the goblin men,
With their shrill repeated cry,
"Come buy, come buy."
When they reached where Laura was,
They stood stock-still upon the moss,
Leering at each other,
Brother with queer brother;
Signalling each other,
Brother with sly brother.
One set his basket down,
One reared his plate;
One began to weave a crown
Of tendrils, leaves, and rough nuts brown
(Men sell not such in any town);
One heaved the golden weight
Of dish and fruit to offer her:
"Come buy, come buy," was still their cry.
Laura stared but did not stir,
Longed, but had no money:
The whisk-tailed merchant bade her taste
In tones as smooth as honey,
The cat-faced purr'd,
The rat-paced spoke a word
Of welcome, and the snail-paced even was heard;
One parrot-voiced and jolly
Cried "Pretty Goblin" still for "Pretty Polly";
One whistled like a bird.

But sweet-tooth Laura spoke in haste:
"Good Folk, I have no coin;
To take were to purloin:
I have no copper in my purse.
I have no silver either,
And all my gold is on the furze
That shakes in windy weather
Above the rusty heather."
"You have much gold upon your head,"
They answered all together:
"Buy from us with a golden curl."
She clipped a precious golden lock,
She dropped a tear more rare than pearl,
Then sucked their fruit globes fair or red:
Sweeter than honey from the rock,
Stronger than man-rejoicing wine,
Clearer than water flowed that juice;
She never tasted such before,
How should it cloy with length of use?
She sucked and sucked and sucked the more
Fruits which that unknown orchard bore;
She sucked until her lips were sore;
Then flung the emptied rinds away
But gathered up one kernel-stone,
And knew not was it night or day
As she turned home alone.

Lizzie met her at the gate
Full of wise upbraidings:
"Dear, you should not stay so late,
Twilight is not good for maidens;
Should not loiter in the glen
In the haunts of goblin men.

Do you not remember Jeanie,
How she met them in the moonlight,
Took their gifts both choice and many,
Ate their fruits and wore their flowers
Plucked from bowers
Where summer ripens at all hours?
But ever in the noonlight
She pined and pined away;
Sought them by night and day,
Found them no more, but dwindled and grew gray;
Then fell with the first snow,
While to this day no grass will grow
Where she lies low:
I planted daisies there a year ago
That never blow.
You should not loiter so."
"Nay, hush," said Laura:
"Nay, hush, my sister:
I ate and ate my fill,
Yet my mouth waters still:
To-morrow night I will
Buy more;" and kissed her:
"Have done with sorrow;
I 'll bring you plums to-morrow
Fresh on their mother twigs,
Cherries worth getting;
You cannot think what figs
My teeth have met in,
What melons icy-cold
Piled on a dish of gold
Too huge for me to hold,
What peaches with a velvet nap,
Pellucid grapes without one seed:

Odorous indeed must be the mead
Whereon they grow, and pure the wave they drink
With lilies at the brink,
And sugar-sweet their sap."

Golden head by golden head,
Like two pigeons in one nest
Folded in each other's wings,
They lay down in their curtained bed:
Like two blossoms on one stem,
Like two flakes of new-fall'n snow,
Like two wands of ivory
Tipped with gold for awful kings.
Moon and stars gazed in at them,
Wind sang to them lullaby,
Lumbering owls forebore to fly,
Not a bat flapped to and fro
Round their nest:
Cheek to cheek and breast to breast
Locked together in one nest.

Early in the morning
When the first cock crowed his warning,
Neat like bees, as sweet and busy,
Laura rose with Lizzie:
Fetched in honey, milked the cows,
Aired and set to rights the house,
Kneaded cakes of whitest wheat,
Cakes for dainty mouths to eat,
Next churned butter, whipped up cream,
Fed their poultry, sat and sewed;
Talked as modest maidens should:
Lizzie with an open heart,

Laura in an absent dream,
One content, one sick in part;
One warbling for the mere bright day's delight,
One longing for the night.

At length slow evening came:
They went with pitchers to the reedy brook;
Lizzie most placid in her look,
Laura most like a leaping flame.
They drew the gurgling water from its deep.
Lizzie plucked purple and rich golden flags,
Then turning homeward said: "The sunset flushes
Those furthest loftiest crags;
Come, Laura, not another maiden lags.
No wilful squirrel wags,
The beasts and birds are fast asleep."
But Laura loitered still among the rushes,
And said the bank was steep.

And said the hour was early still,
The dew not fall'n, the wind not chill;
Listening ever, but not catching
The customary cry,
"Come buy, come buy,"
With its iterated jingle
Of sugar-baited words:
Not for all her watching
Once discerning even one goblin
Racing, whisking, tumbling, hobbling;
Let alone the herds
That used to tramp along the glen,
In groups or single,
Of brisk fruit-merchant men.

O
LAURA
COME.

Till Lizzie urged, "O Laura, come;
I hear the fruit-call, but I dare not look:
You should not loiter longer at this brook:
Come with me home.
The stars rise, the moon bends her arc,
Each glow-worm winks her spark,
Let us get home before the night grows dark:
For clouds may gather
Though this is summer weather,
Put out the lights and drench us through;
Then if we lost our way what should we do?"

Laura turned cold as stone
To find her sister heard that cry alone,
That goblin cry,
"Come buy our fruits, come buy."
Must she then buy no more such dainty fruits?
Must she no more such succous pasture find,
Gone deaf and blind?
Her tree of life drooped from the root:
She said not one word in her heart's sore ache:
But peering thro' the dimness, nought discerning,
Trudged home, her pitcher dripping all the way;
So crept to bed, and lay
Silent till Lizzie slept;
Then sat up in a passionate yearning,
And gnashed her teeth for baulked desire, and wept
As if her heart would break.

Day after day, night after night,
Laura kept watch in vain
In sullen silence of exceeding pain.
She never caught again the goblin cry,

"Come buy, come buy;"—
She never spied the goblin men
Hawking their fruits along the glen:
But when the moon waxed bright
Her hair grew thin and gray;
She dwindled, as the fair full moon doth turn
To swift decay and burn
Her fire away.

One day remembering her kernel-stone
She set it by a wall that faced the south;
Dewed it with tears, hoped for a root,
Watched for a waxing shoot,
But there came none.
It never saw the sun,
It never felt the trickling moisture run:
While with sunk eyes and faded mouth
She dreamed of melons, as a traveller sees
False waves in desert drouth
With shade of leaf-crowned trees,
And burns the thirstier in the sandful breeze.

She no more swept the house,
Tended the fowls or cows,
Fetched honey, kneaded cakes of wheat,
Brought water from the brook:
But sat down listless in the chimney-nook
And would not eat.

Tender Lizzie could not bear
To watch her sister's cankerous care,
Yet not to share.
She night and morning

Caught the goblins' cry:
"Come buy our orchard fruits,
Come buy, come buy:"—
Beside the brook, along the glen,
She heard the tramp of goblin men,
The voice and stir
Poor Laura could not hear;
Longed to buy fruit to comfort her,
But feared to pay too dear.
She thought of Jeanie in her grave,
Who should have been a bride;
But who for joys brides hope to have
Fell sick and died
In her gay prime,
In earliest Winter time,
With the first glazing rime,
With the first snow-fall of crisp Winter time.

Till Laura dwindling
Seemed knocking at Death's door:
Then Lizzie weighed no more
Better and worse;
But put a silver penny in her purse,
Kissed Laura, crossed the heath with clumps of furze
At twilight, halted by the brook:
And for the first time in her life
Began to listen and look.

Laughed every goblin
When they spied her peeping:
Came towards her hobbling,
Flying, running, leaping,

Puffing and blowing
Chuckling, clapping, crowing,
Clucking and gobbling,
Moping and mowing,
Full of airs and graces,
Pulling wry faces,
Demure grimaces,
Cat-like and rat-like,
Ratel- and wombat-like,
Snail-paced in a hurry,
Parrot-voiced and whistler,
Helter skelter, hurry skurry,
Chattering like magpies,
Fluttering like pigeons,
Gliding like fishes,—
Hugged her and kissed her:
Squeezed and caressed her:
Stretched up their dishes,
Panniers, and plates:
"Look at our apples
Russet and dun,
Bob at our cherries,
Bite at our peaches,
Citrons and dates,
Grapes for the asking,
Pears red with basking
Out in the sun,
Plums on their twigs;
Pluck them and suck them,
Pomegranates, figs."—

"Good folk," said Lizzie,
Mindful of Jeanie:

"Give me much and many:"
Held out her apron,
Tossed them her penny.
"Nay, take a seat with us,
Honour and eat with us,"
They answered grinning:
"Our feast is but beginning.
Night yet is early,
Warm and dew-pearly,
Wakeful and starry:
Such fruits as these
No man can carry;
Half their bloom would fly,
Half their dew would dry,
Half their flavour would pass by.
Sit down and feast with us,
Be welcome guest with us,
Cheer you and rest with us."—
"Thank you," said Lizzie: "But one waits
At home alone for me:
So without further parleying,
If you will not sell me any
Of your fruits though much and many
Give me back my silver penny
I tossed you for a fee."—
They began to scratch their pates,
No longer wagging, purring,
But visibly demurring,
Grunting and snarling.
One called her proud,
Cross-grained, uncivil;
Their tones waxed loud,
Their looks were evil.

Lashing their tails
They trod and hustled her,
Elbowed and jostled her,
Clawed with their nails,
Barking, mewing, hissing, mocking,
Tore her gown and soiled her stocking,
Twitched her hair out by the roots,
Stamped upon her tender feet,
Held her hands and squeezed their fruits
Against her mouth to make her eat.

White and golden Lizzie stood,
Like a lily in a flood,—
Like a rock of blue-veined stone
Lashed by tides obstreperously,—
Like a beacon left alone
In a hoary roaring sea,
Sending up a golden fire,—
Like a fruit-crowned orange-tree
White with blossoms honey-sweet
Sore beset by wasp and bee,—
Like a royal virgin town
Topped with gilded dome and spire
Close beleaguered by a fleet
Mad to tug her standard down.

One may lead a horse to water,
Twenty cannot make him drink.
Though the goblins cuffed and caught her,
Coaxed and fought her,
Bullied and besought her,
Scratched her, pinched her black as ink,
Kicked and knocked her,

WHITE·AND·
GOLDEN
·LIZZIE·STOOD

Mauled and mocked her,
Lizzie uttered not a word;
Would not open lip from lip
Lest they should cram a mouthful in:
But laughed in heart to feel the drip
Of juice that syruped all her face,
And lodged in dimples of her chin,
And streaked her neck which quaked like curd.
At last the evil people,
Worn out by her resistance,
Flung back her penny, kicked their fruit
Along whichever road they took,
Not leaving root or stone or shoot;
Some writhed into the ground,
Some dived into the brook
With ring and ripple,
Some scudded on the gale without a sound,
Some vanished in the distance.

In a smart, ache, tingle,
Lizzie went her way;
Knew not was it night or day;
Sprang up the bank, tore thro' the furze,
Threaded copse and dingle,
And heard her penny jingle
Bouncing in her purse,—
Its bounce was music to her ear.
She ran and ran
As if she feared some goblin man
Dogged her with gibe or curse
Or something worse:
But not one goblin skurried after,
Nor was she pricked by fear;

The kind heart made her windy-paced
That urged her home quite out of breath with haste
And inward laughter.

She cried, "Laura," up the garden,
"Did you miss me?
Come and kiss me.
Never mind my bruises,
Hug me, kiss me, suck my juices
Squeezed from goblin fruits for you,
Goblin pulp and goblin dew.
Eat me, drink me, love me;
Laura, make much of me:
For your sake I have braved the glen
And had to do with goblin merchant men."

Laura started from her chair,
Flung her arms up in the air,
Clutched her hair:
"Lizzie, Lizzie, have you tasted
For my sake the fruit forbidden?
Must your light like mine be hidden,
Your young life like mine be wasted,
Undone in mine undoing,
And ruined in my ruin,
Thirsty, cankered, goblin-ridden?"—
She clung about her sister,
Kissed and kissed and kissed her:
Tears once again
Refreshed her shrunken eyes,
Dropping like rain
After long sultry drouth;

Shaking with aguish fear, and pain,
She kissed and kissed her with a hungry mouth.

Her lips began to scorch,
That juice was wormwood to her tongue,
She loathed the feast:
Writhing as one possessed she leaped and sung,
Rent all her robe, and wrung
Her hands in lamentable haste,
And beat her breast.
Her locks streamed like the torch
Borne by a racer at full speed,
Or like the mane of horses in their flight,
Or like an eagle when she stems the light
Straight toward the sun,
Or like a caged thing freed,
Or like a flying flag when armies run.

Swift fire spread through her veins, knocked at her heart,
Met the fire smouldering there
And overbore its lesser flame;
She gorged on bitterness without a name:
Ah! fool, to choose such part
Of soul-consuming care!
Sense failed in the mortal strife:
Like the watch-tower of a town
Which an earthquake shatters down,
Like a lightning-stricken mast,
Like a wind-uprooted tree
Spun about,
Like a foam-topped waterspout

Cast down headlong in the sea,
She fell at last;
Pleasure past and anguish past,
Is it death or is it life?

Life out of death.
That night long Lizzie watched by her,
Counted her pulse's flagging stir,
Felt for her breath,
Held water to her lips, and cooled her face
With tears and fanning leaves:
But when the first birds chirped about their eaves,
And early reapers plodded to the place
Of golden sheaves,
And dew-wet grass
Bowed in the morning winds so brisk to pass,
And new buds with new day
Opened of cup-like lilies on the stream,
Laura awoke as from a dream,
Laughed in the innocent old way,
Hugged Lizzie but not twice or thrice;
Her gleaming locks showed not one thread of gray,
Her breath was sweet as May,
And light danced in her eyes.

Days, weeks, months, years,
Afterwards, when both were wives
With children of their own;
Their mother-hearts beset with fears,
Their lives bound up in tender lives;
Laura would call the little ones
And tell them of her early prime,
Those pleasant days long gone

Of not-returning time:
Would talk about the haunted glen,
The wicked, quaint fruit-merchant men.
Their fruits like honey to the throat
But poison in the blood;
(Men sell not such in any town:)
Would tell them how her sister stood
In deadly peril to do her good,
And win the fiery antidote:
Then joining hands to little hands
Would bid them cling together,
"For there is no friend like a sister
In calm or stormy weather;
To cheer one on the tedious way,
To fetch one if one goes astray,
To lift one if one totters down,
To strengthen whilst one stands."

THE HOUR AND THE GHOST

Bride

O LOVE, love, hold me fast,
He draws me away from thee;
I cannot stem the blast,
Nor the cold strong sea:
Far away a light shines
Beyond the hills and pines;
It is lit for me.

Bridegroom

I have thee close, my dear,
No terror can come near;
Only far off the northern light shines clear.

Ghost

Come with me, fair and false,
To our home, come home.
It is my voice that calls:

Once thou wast not afraid
When I wooed, and said,
"Come, our nest is newly made"—
Now cross the tossing foam.

Bride

Hold me one moment longer,
He taunts me with the past,
His clutch is waxing stronger,
Hold me fast, hold me fast.
He draws me from thy heart,
And I cannot withhold:
He bids my spirit depart
With him into the cold:—
Oh bitter vows of old!

Bridegroom

Lean on me, hide thine eyes:
Only ourselves, earth and skies,
Are present here: be wise.

Ghost

Lean on me, come away,
I will guide and steady:
Come, for I will not stay:
Come, for house and bed are ready.
Ah, sure bed and house,
For better and worse, for life and death;
Goal won with shortened breath:
Come, crown our vows.

Bride

One moment, one more word,
While my heart beats still,
While my breath is stirred
By my fainting will.
O friend, forsake me not,
Forget not as I forgot:
But keep thy heart for me,
Keep thy faith true and bright;
Through the lone cold winter night
Perhaps I may come to thee.

Bridegroom

Nay peace, my darling, peace:
Let these dreams and terrors cease:
Who spoke of death or change or aught but ease?

Ghost

O fair frail sin,
O poor harvest gathered in!
Thou shalt visit him again
To watch his heart grow cold;
To know the gnawing pain
I knew of old;
To see one much more fair
Fill up the vacant chair,
Fill his heart, his children bear:—
While thou and I together
In the outcast weather
Toss and howl and spin.

"Come with me, fair and false"

The Hour and the Ghost.

MY DREAM

HEAR now a curious dream I dreamed last night,
Each word whereof is weighed and sifted truth.

I stood beside Euphrates while it swelled
Like overflowing Jordan in its youth:
It waxed and coloured sensibly to sight;
Till out of myriad pregnant waves there welled
Young crocodiles, a gaunt blunt-featured crew,
Fresh-hatched perhaps and daubed with birthday dew.
The rest if I should tell, I fear my friend,
My closest friend, would deem the facts untrue;
And therefore it were wisely left untold;
Yet if you will, why hear it to the end.

Each crocodile was girt with massive gold
And polished stones that with their wearers grew:
But one there was who waxed beyond the rest,
Wore kinglier girdle and a kingly crown,

Whilst crowns and orbs and sceptres starred his breast.
All gleamed compact and green with scale on scale,
But special burnishment adorned his mail
And special terror weighed upon his frown;
His punier brethren quaked before his tail,
Broad as a rafter, potent as a flail.
So he grew lord and master of his kin:
But who shall tell the tale of all their woes?
An execrable appetite arose,
He battened on them, crunched, and sucked them in
He knew no law, he feared no binding law,
But ground them with inexorable jaw:
The luscious fat distilled upon his chin,
Exuded from his nostrils and his eyes,
While still like hungry death he fed his maw;
Till every minor crocodile being dead
And buried too, himself gorged to the full,
He slept with breath oppressed and unstrung claw.
Oh marvel passing strange which next I saw:
In sleep he dwindled to the common size,
And all the empire faded from his coat.
Then from far off a wingèd vessel came,
Swift as a swallow, subtle as a flame:
I know not what it bore of freight or host,
But white it was as an avenging ghost.
It levelled strong Euphrates in its course;
Supreme yet weightless as an idle mote
It seemed to tame the waters without force
Till not a murmur swelled or billow beat:
Lo, as the purple shadow swept the sands,
The prudent crocodile rose on his feet,
And shed appropriate tears and wrung his hands.

What can it mean? you ask. I answer not
For meaning, but myself must echo, What?
And tell it as I saw it on the spot.

A ROYAL PRINCESS

I a Princess king-descended, stuck with jewels, gilded, dressed,
Would rather be a peasant with her baby at her breast,
For all I shine so like the sun, and am purple like the west.

Two and two my guards behind, two and two before,
Two and two on either hand, they guard me evermore;
Me, poor dove that must not coo—eagle that must not soar.

All my fountains cast up perfumes, all my gardens grow
Scented woods and foreign spices, with all flowers in blow
That are costly, out of season as the seasons go.

All my walls are lost in mirrors, whereupon I trace
Self to right hand, self to left hand, self in every place,
Self-same solitary figure, self-same seeking face.

Then I have an ivory chair high to sit upon,
Almost like my Father's chair which is an ivory throne:
There I sit uplift and upright, there I sit alone.

Alone by day, alone by night, alone days without end;
My Father and my Mother give me treasures, search and spend:—
O my Father, O my Mother, have you ne'er a friend?

As I am a lofty princess, so my Father is
A lofty king, accomplished in all kingly subtilties,
Holding in his strong right hand world-kingdoms' balances.

He has quarrelled with his neighbours, he has scourged his foes;
Vassal counts and princes follow where his pennon goes,
Long-descended valiant lords whom the vulture knows,

On whose track the vulture swoops, when they ride in state
To break the strength of armies and topple down the great:
Each of these my courteous servant, none of these my mate.

My Father counting up his strength sets down with equal pen
So many head of cattle, head of horses, head of men:
These for slaughter, these for breeding, with the how and when.

Some to work on roads, canals, some to man his ships;
Some to smart in mines beneath sharp overseers' whips;
Some to trap fur-beasts in lands where utmost winter nips.

Once it came into my heart, and whelmed me like a flood,
That these too are men and women, human flesh and blood;
Men with hearts and men with souls, tho' trodden down like mud.

All that day I sat alone, would not eat nor drink,
Sat humiliated down in dust to weep and think:
My heart grew like a stone; I felt it sink and sink and sink.

At night my Father held a banquet; I must needs be there,
Statue-cold, severe, and stately, if not statue-fair;
With hereditary jewels clustered in my hair,

With a fan of rainbow feathers and a golden chain;
Some bore gusty lights before me, some bore up my train:
"These are men, are men, are men," throbbed my heart and brain.

Our feasting was not glad that night, our music was not gay;
On my Mother's graceful head I marked a thread of gray,
My father frowning at the fare seemed every dish to weigh.

I sat beside them sole princess in my exalted place,
My ladies and my gentlemen stood by me on the dais:
A mirror showed me I look old and haggard in the face;

It showed me that my ladies all are fair to gaze upon,
Plump, plenteous-haired, to every one love's secret lore is known,
They laugh by day, they sleep by night: ah me, what is a throne?

The singing men and women sang that night as usual,
The dancers danced in pairs and sets; but music had a fall,
A melancholy windy fall as at a funeral.

Amid the toss of torches to my chamber back we swept;
My ladies loosed my golden chain; meantime I could have wept
To think of one that was not loosed whether I waked or slept.

I took my bath of scented milk delicately waited on,
They burned sweet things for my delight, cedar and cinnamon,
They lit my shaded silver lamp and left me there alone.

A day went by, a week went by; and next I heard it said:
"Men are clamouring, women, children, clamouring to be fed;
Men, like famished dogs, are howling in the streets for bread."

So two whispered by my door, not thinking I could hear,
Vulgar, naked truth, ungarnished for a royal ear;
Fit for hustling in the background, not to stalk so near.

But I strained my utmost sense to catch this truth and mark:—
"There are families out grazing like cattle in the park."—
"A pair of peasants must be saved, even if we build an ark."

A merry jest, a merry laugh; each strolled upon his way:
One was my page, a pretty lad, in dress perhaps too gay;
One was my youngest maid, as sweet and white as cream in May.

Other footsteps followed softly with a weightier tramp;
Voices said: "Picked soldiers have been summoned from the camp,
To quell these base-born ruffians who make free to howl and stamp."

"Howl and stamp?" one answered: "They made free to hurl a stone
At the minister's state coach, well aimed and stoutly thrown."
"There 's work then for the soldiers, for this rank crop must be mown."

"One I saw, a poor old fool with ashes on his head,
Whimpering because a girl had snatched his crust of bread:
Then he dropped; when some one raised him, it turned out he was dead."

"After us the deluge," was retorted with a laugh:
"If bread 's the staff of life they must walk without a staff."—
"While I 've a loaf they 're welcome to my blessing and the chaff."—

These passed. The king: stand up. Said my father with a smile:
"Daughter mine, your mother comes to sit with you awhile,
She's sad to-day; and who but you her sadness can beguile?"

He too left me. Shall I touch my harp now while I wait,—
I hear them doubling guard below before our palace gate—
Or shall I work the last gold stitch into my veil of state;

Or shall my woman stand and read some unimpassioned scene,
There's music of a lulling sort in words that pause between;
Or shall she merely fan me while I wait here for the queen?

Again I caught my father's voice in sharp words of command:
"Charge"—a clash of steel:—"Charge again, the rebels stand.
Smite and spare not, hand to hand; smite and spare not, hand to hand."

There swelled a tumult at the gate, high voices waxing higher;
A flash of red reflected light lit the cathedral spire;
I heard a cry for faggots, then I heard a yell for fire.

"Sit and roast there with your meat, sit and bake there with your bread,
You who sat and saw us starve," one shrieking woman said:
"Sit on your throne and roast with your crown upon your head."

O Queen my Mother, come in haste; yet is your haste too slack;
I have set my face towards where there is no looking back,
I have set my foot upon the unreturning track.

This thing will I do, whilst my mother tarrieth:
I will take my fine spun gold, but not to sew therewith;
I will take my gold and gems, and rainbow fan and wreath;

I, if I perish, perish

A Royal Princess.

With a ransom in my lap, a king's ransom in my hand,
I will go down to the people, will stand face to face; will stand
Where they curse King, Queen, and Princess of this cursed land.

They shall take all to buy them bread, take all I have to give;
I, if I perish, perish; they to-day shall eat and live;
I, if I perish, perish, that 's the goal I half conceive:

Once to stand up face to face with heart-pulse loud and hot—
It may be in this latter day I stand thus in my lot—
And say: "I love you, love you," to those who know me not;

Once to speak before the world, rend bare my heart and show
The lesson I have learned, which is death, is life, to know.
I, if I perish, perish. In the name of God I go.

MY heart is like a singing bird
  Whose nest is in a watered shoot;
My heart is like an apple-tree
  Whose boughs are bent with thickset fruit;
My heart is like a rainbow shell
  That paddles in a halcyon sea;
My heart is gladder than all these
  Because my love is come to me.

Raise me a dais of silk and down;
  Hang it with vair and purple dyes;
Carve it in doves, and pomegranates,
  And peacocks with a hundred eyes;
Work it in gold and silver grapes,
  In leaves, and silver fleurs-de-lys;
Because the birthday of my life
  Is come, my love is come to me.

MAUDE CLARE

THE fields were white with lily-buds
  White gleamed the lilied beck;
Each mated pigeon plumed the pomp
  Of his metallic neck.

She follow'd his bride into the church
  With a lofty step and mien:
His bride was like a village maid,
  Maude Clare was like a queen.

The minstrels made loud marriage din;
  Each guest sat in his place,
To eat and drink, and wish good luck,
  To do the wedding grace;

To eat and drink, and wish good luck,
  To sing, and laugh, and jest:
One only neither ate nor drank,
  Nor clapp'd her hands, nor bless'd.

"Son Thomas," his lady mother said,
  With smiles, almost with tears,
"May Nell and you but live as true
  As we have done for years;

"Your father thirty years ago
  Had just your tale to tell;
But he was not so pale as you,
  Nor I so pale as Nell."

My lord was pale with inward strife,
  And Nell was pale with pride;
My lord gazed long on pale Maude Clare
  Or ever he kiss'd the bride.

No eyes were fix'd upon the bride,
  Or on the bridegroom more,
All eyes were fix'd on grand Maude Clare
  While she look'd straight before.

"Lo, I have brought my gift, my lord,
  Have brought my gift," she said—
"To bless the hearth, to bless the board,
  To bless the marriage-bed.

"Here's my half of the golden chain
  You wore about your neck,
That day we waded ankle-deep
  For lilies in the beck:

"Here's my half of the faded leaves
  We pluck'd from budding bough,
With feet amongst the lily leaves,—
  The lilies are budding now."

HERE'S·MY·HALF·OF·
THE·GOLDEN·CHAIN·

He strove to match her scorn with scorn,
  He falter'd in his place:
"Lady," he said,—"Maude Clare," he said,
  "Maude Clare,"—and hid his face.

She turned to Nell: "My Lady Nell,
  I have a gift for you;
Though, were it fruit, the bloom were gone,
  Or, were it flowers, the dew.

"Take my share of a fickle heart,
  Mine of a paltry love:
Take it or leave it as you will,
  I wash my hands thereof."

"And what you leave," said Nell, "I 'll take,
  And what you spurn I 'll wear;
For he 's my lord for better and worse,
  And him I love, Maude Clare.

"Yea though you 're taller by the head
  More wise, and much more fair,
I 'll love him till he loves me best—
  Me best of all, Maude Clare."

THE first was like a dream through summer heat,
  The second like a tedious numbing swoon,
While the half-frozen pulses lagged to beat
  Beneath a winter moon.

"But," says my friend, "what was this thing and where?"
  It was a pleasure-place within my soul;
An earthly paradise supremely fair
  That lured me from the goal.

The first part was a tissue of hugged lies;
  The second was its ruin fraught with pain:
Why raise the fair delusion to the skies
  But to be dashed again?

My castle stood of white transparent glass
  Glittering and frail with many a fretted spire.
But when the summer sunset came to pass
  It kindled into fire.

My castle stood of white transparent glass

From House to Home.

My pleasaunce was an undulating green,
  Stately with trees whose shadows slept below,
With glimpses of smooth garden-beds between
  Like flame or sky or snow.

Swift squirrels on the pastures took their ease,
  With leaping lambs safe from the unfeared knife;
All singing-birds rejoicing in those trees
  Fulfilled their careless life.

Wood-pigeons cooed there, stock-doves nestled there;
  My trees were full of songs and flowers and fruit,
Their branches spread a city to the air,
  And mice lodged in their root.

My heath lay farther off, where lizards lived
  In strange metallic mail, just spied and gone;
Like darted lightnings here and there perceived
  But nowhere dwelt upon.

Frogs and fat toads were there to hop or plod
  And propagate in peace, an uncouth crew,
Where velvet-headed rushes rustling nod
  And spill the morning dew.

All caterpillars throve beneath my rule,
  With snails and slugs in corners out of sight;
I never marred the curious sudden stool
  That perfects in a night.

Safe in his excavated gallery
  The burrowing mole groped on from year to year;
No harmless hedgehog curled because of me
  His prickly back for fear.

Oft-times one like an angel walked with me,
  With spirit-discerning eyes like flames of fire,
But deep as the unfathomed endless sea,
  Fulfilling my desire:

And sometimes like a snowdrift he was fair,
  And sometimes like a sunset glorious red,
And sometimes he had wings to scale the air
  With aureole round his head.

We sang our songs together by the way,
  Calls and recalls and echoes of delight;
So communed we together all the day,
  And so in dreams by night.

I have no words to tell what way we walked,
  What unforgotten path now closed and sealed:
I have no words to tell all things we talked,
  All things that he revealed:

This only can I tell: that hour by hour
  I waxed more feastful, lifted up and glad;
I felt no thorn-prick when I plucked a flower,
  Felt not my friend was sad.

"To-morrow," once I said to him with smiles:
  "To-night," he answered gravely; and was dumb,
But pointed out the stones that numbered miles
  And miles and miles to come.

"Not so," I said: "to-morrow shall be sweet;
  To-night is not so sweet as coming days."
Then first I saw that he had turned his feet,
  Had turned from me his face:

Running and flying miles and miles he went,
  But once looked back to beckon with his hand,
And cry: "Come home, O love, from banishment:
  Come to the distant land."

That night destroyed me like an avalanche;
  One night turned all my summer back to snow:
Next morning not a bird upon my branch,
  Not a lamb woke below,—

No bird, no lamb, no living breathing thing;
  No squirrel scampered on my breezy lawn,
No mouse lodged by his hoard: all joys took wing
  And fled before that dawn.

Azure and sun were starved from heaven above,
  No dew had fallen, but biting frost lay hoar:
O love, I knew that I should meet my love,
  Should find my love no more.

"My love no more," I muttered, stunned with pain:
  I shed no tear, I wrung no passionate hand,
Till something whispered: "You shall meet again,
  Meet in a distant land."

Then with a cry like famine I arose,
  I lit my candle, searched from room to room,
Searched up and down; a war of winds that froze
  Swept through the blank of gloom.

I searched day after day, night after night;
  Scant change there came to me of night or day:
"No more," I wailed, "no more:" and trimmed my light,
  And gnashed but did not pray,

Until my heart broke and my spirit broke:
  Upon the frost-bound floor I stumbled, fell,
And moaned: "It is enough: withhold the stroke.
  Farewell, O love, farewell."

Then life swooned from me. And I heard the song
  Of spheres and spirits rejoicing over me:
One cried: "Our sister, she hath suffered long."—
  One answered: "Make her see."—

One cried: "Oh blessèd she who no more pain,
  Who no more disappointment shall receive."—
One answered: "Not so: she must live again;
  Strengthen thou her to live."

So while I lay entranced a curtain seemed
  To shrivel with crackling from before my face:
Across mine eyes a waxing radiance beamed
  And showed a certain place.

I saw a vision of a woman, where
  Night and new morning strive for domination;
Incomparably pale, and almost fair,
  And sad beyond expression.

Her eyes were like some fire-enshrining gem,
  Were stately like the stars, and yet were tender;
Her figure charmed me like a windy stem
  Quivering and drooped and slender.

I stood upon the outer barren ground,
  She stood on inner ground that budded flowers;
While circling in their never-slackening round
  Danced by the mystic hours.

She stood on inner ground that budded flowers

From House to Home.

But every flower was lifted on a thorn,
  And every thorn shot upright from its sands
To gall her feet; hoarse laughter pealed in scorn
  With cruel clapping hands.

She bled and wept, yet did not shrink; her strength
  Was strung up until daybreak of delight:
She measured measureless sorrow toward its length,
  And breadth, and depth, and height.

Then marked I how a chain sustained her form,
  A chain of living links not made nor riven:
It stretched sheer up through lightning, wind, and storm,
  And anchored fast in heaven.

One cried: "How long? yet founded on the Rock
  She shall do battle, suffer, and attain."—
One answered: "Faith quakes in the tempest shock:
  Strengthen her soul again."

I saw a cup sent down and come to her
  Brimfull of loathing and of bitterness:
She drank with livid lips that seemed to stir
  The depth, not make it less.

But as she drank I spied a hand distil
  New wine and virgin honey; making it
First bitter-sweet, then sweet indeed, until
  She tasted only sweet.

Her lips and cheeks waxed rosy-fresh and young;
  Drinking she sang "My soul shall nothing want;"
And drank anew: while soft a song was sung,
  A mystical slow chant.

One cried: "The wounds are faithful of a friend:
  The wilderness shall blossom as a rose."—
One answered: "Rend the veil, declare the end,
  Strengthen her ere she goes."

Then earth and heaven were rolled up like a scroll;
  Time and space, change and death, had passed away;
Weight, number, measure, each had reached its whole;
  The day had come, that day.

Multitudes—multitudes—stood up in bliss,
  Made equal to the angels, glorious, fair;
With harps, palms, wedding-garments, kiss of peace,
  And crowned and haloed hair.

They sang a song, a new song in the height,
  Harping with harps to Him Who is Strong and True:
They drank new wine, their eyes saw with new light,
  Lo, all things were made new.

Tier beyond tier they rose and rose and rose,
  So high that it was dreadful, flames with flames:
No man could number them, no tongue disclose
  Their secret sacred names.

As though one pulse stirred all, one rush of blood
  Fed all, one breath swept through them myriad-voiced,
They struck their harps, cast down their crowns, they stood
  And worshipped and rejoiced.

Each face looked one way like a moon new-lit,
  Each face looked one way towards its Sun of Love;
Drank love and bathed in love and mirrored it
  And knew no end thereof.

Glory touched glory on each blessèd head,
  Hands locked dear hands never to sunder more:
These were the new-begotten from the dead
  Whom the great birthday bore.

Heart answered heart, soul answered soul at rest,
  Double against each other, filled, sufficed:
All loving, loved of all; but loving best
  And best beloved of Christ.

I saw that one who lost her love in pain,
  Who trod on thorns, who drank the loathsome cup;
The lost in night, in day was found again;
  The fallen was lifted up.

They stood together in the blessèd noon,
  They sang together through the length of days;
Each loving face bent Sunwards like a moon
  New-lit with love and praise.

Therefore, O friend, I would not if I might
  Rebuild my house of lies, wherein I joyed
One time to dwell: my soul shall walk in white,
  Cast down but not destroyed.

Therefore in patience I possess my soul;
  Yea, therefore as a flint I set my face,
To pluck down, to build up again the whole—
  But in a distant place.

These thorns are sharp, yet I can tread on them;
  This cup is loathsome, yet He makes it sweet:
My face is steadfast toward Jerusalem,
  My heart remembers it.

I lift the hanging hands, the feeble knees—
  I, precious more than seven times molten gold—
Until the day when from His storehouses
  God shall bring new and old;

Beauty for ashes, oil of joy for grief,
  Garment of praise for spirit of heaviness:
Although to-day I fade as doth a leaf,
  I languish and grow less.

Although to-day He prunes my twigs with pain,
  Yet doth His blood nourish and warm my root:
To-morrow I shall put forth buds again
  And clothe myself with fruit.

Although to-day I walk in tedious ways,
  To-day His staff is turned into a rod,
Yet will I wait for Him the appointed days
  And stay upon my God.

GOES·SINGING·
AS·IT·LEAPS·
ALONG.

A BLUE-EYED phantom far before
  Is laughing, leaping toward the sun:
Like lead I chase it evermore,
  I pant and run.

It breaks the sunlight bound on bound:
  Goes singing as it leaps along
To sheep-bells with a dreamy sound
  A dreamy song.

I laugh, it is so brisk and gay;
  It is so far before, I weep:
I hope I shall lie down some day,
  Lie down and sleep.

SOUND the deep waters:—
  Who shall sound that deep?—
Too short the plummet,
  And the watchmen sleep.
Some dream of effort
  Up a toilsome steep;
Some dream of pasture grounds
  For harmless sheep.

White shapes flit to and fro
  From mast to mast;
They feel the distant tempest
  That nears them fast:
Great rocks are straight ahead,
  Great shoals not past;
They shout to one another
  Upon the blast.

Pale spirits, wailing

Sleep at Sea.

Sleep at Sea

Oh, soft the streams drop music
  Between the hills,
And musical the birds' nests
  Beside those rills:
The nests are types of home
  Love-hidden from ills,
The nests are types of spirits
  Love-music fills.

So dream the sleepers,
  Each man in his place;
The lightning shows the smile
  Upon each face:
The ship is driving, driving,
  It drives apace:
And sleepers smile, and spirits
  Bewail their case.

The lightning glares and reddens
  Across the skies;
It seems but sunset
  To those sleeping eyes.
When did the sun go down
  On such a wise?
From such a sunset
  When shall day arise?

"Wake," call the spirits:
  But to heedless ears:
They have forgotten sorrows
  And hopes and fears;
They have forgotten perils
  And smiles and tears;

Their dream has held them long,
Long years and years.

"Wake," call the spirits again:
But it would take
A louder summons
To bid them awake.
Some dream of pleasure
For another's sake:
Some dream, forgetful
Of a lifelong ache.

One by one slowly,
Ah, how sad and slow!
Wailing and praying
The spirits rise and go:
Clear stainless spirits,
White as white as snow;
Pale spirits, wailing
For an overthrow.

One by one flitting,
Like a mournful bird
Whose song is tired at last
For no mate heard.
The loving voice is silent,
The useless word;
One by one flitting
Sick with hope deferred.

Driving and driving,
The ship drives amain:

While swift from mast to mast
  Shapes flit again,
Flit silent as the silence
  Where men lie slain;
Their shadow cast upon the sails
  Is like a stain.

No voice to call the sleepers,
  No hand to raise:
They sleep to death in dreaming
  Of length of days.
Vanity of vanities,
  The Preacher says:
Vanity is the end
  Of all their ways.

REPINING

SHE sat alway thro' the long day
Spinning the weary thread away;
And ever said in undertone:
"Come, that I be no more alone."

From early dawn to set of sun
Working, her task was still undone;
And the long thread seemed to increase
Even while she spun and did not cease.
She heard the gentle turtle-dove
Tell to its mate a tale of love;
She saw the glancing swallows fly,
Ever a social company;
She knew each bird upon its nest
Had cheering songs to bring it rest;
None lived alone save only she;—
The wheel went round more wearily;
She wept and said in undertone:
"Come, that I be no more alone."

"Ah woe is me!"

Repining.

Day followed day and still she sighed
For love, and was not satisfied;
Until one night, when the moonlight
Turned all the trees to silver-white,
She heard, what ne'er she heard before,
A steady hand undo the door.
The nightingale since set of sun
Her throbbing music had not done,
And she had listened silently;
But now the wind had changed, and she
Heard the sweet song no more, but heard
Beside her bed a whispered word:
"Damsel, rise up; be not afraid;
For I am come at last," it said.

She trembled, tho' the voice was mild;
She trembled like a frightened child;—
Till she looked up, and then she saw
The unknown speaker without awe.
He seemed a fair young man, his eyes
Beaming with serious charities;
His cheek was white but hardly pale;
And a dim glory like a veil
Hovered about his head, and shone
Thro' the whole room till night was gone.

So her fear fled; and then she said,
Leaning upon her quiet bed:
"Now thou art come, I prithee stay,
That I may see thee in the day,
And learn to know thy voice, and hear
It evermore calling me near."

He answered: "Rise and follow me."
But she looked upwards wonderingly:
"And whither wouldst thou go, friend? stay
Until the dawning of the day."
But he said: "The wind ceaseth, Maid;
Of chill nor damp be thou afraid."

She bound her hair up from the floor,
And passed in silence from the door.

So they went forth together, he
Helping her forward tenderly.
The hedges bowed beneath his hand;
Forth from the streams came the dry land
As they passed over; evermore
The pallid moonbeams shone before;
And the wind hushed, and nothing stirred;
Not even a solitary bird,
Scared by their footsteps, fluttered by
Where aspen-trees stood steadily.

As they went on, at length a sound
Came trembling on the air around;
The undistinguishable hum
Of life, voices that go and come
Of busy men, and the child's sweet
High laugh, and noise of trampling feet.

Then he said, "Wilt thou go and see?"
And she made answer joyfully;
"The noise of life, of human life,
Of dear communion without strife,

SO·THEY·WENT·
FORTH·TOGETHER·

Of converse held 'twixt friend and friend;
Is it not here our path shall end?"
He led her on a little way
Until they reached a hillock: "Stay."

It was a village in a plain.
High mountains screened it from the rain
And stormy wind; and nigh at hand
A bubbling streamlet flowed, o'er sand
Pebbly and fine, and sent life up
Green succous stalk and flower-cup.

Gradually, day's harbinger,
A chilly wind began to stir.
It seemed a gentle powerless breeze
That scarcely rustled thro' the trees;
And yet it touched the mountain's head
And the paths man might never tread.
But hearken: in the quiet weather
Do all the streams flow down together?—

No, 'tis a sound more terrible
Than tho' a thousand rivers fell.
The everlasting ice and snow
Were loosened then, but not to flow;—
With a loud crash like solid thunder
The avalanche came, burying under
The village; turning life and breath
And rest and joy and plans to death.

"Oh! let us fly, for pity fly;
Let us go hence, friend, thou and I.
There must be many regions yet
Where these things make not desolate."

He looked upon her seriously;
Then said: "Arise and follow me."
The path that lay before them was
Nigh covered over with long grass;
And many slimy things and slow
Trailed on between the roots below.
The moon looked dimmer than before;
And shadowy cloudlets floating o'er
Its face sometimes quite hid its light,
And filled the skies with deeper night.

At last, as they went on, the noise
Was heard of the sea's mighty voice;
And soon the ocean could be seen
In its long restlessness serene.
Upon its breast a vessel rode
That drowsily appeared to nod
As the great billows rose and fell,
And swelled to sink, and sank to swell.

Meanwhile the strong wind had come forth
From the chill regions of the North,
The mighty wind invisible.
And the low waves began to swell;
And the sky darkened overhead;
And the moon once looked forth, then fled
Behind dark clouds; while here and there
The lightning shone out in the air;
And the approaching thunder rolled
With angry pealings manifold.
How many vows were made, and prayers
That in safe times were cold and scarce.

Still all availed not; and at length
The waves arose in all their strength,
And fought against the ship, and filled
The ship. Then were the clouds unsealed,
And the rain hurried forth, and beat
On every side and over it.

Some clung together, and some kept
A long stern silence, and some wept.
Many half crazed looked on in wonder
As the strong timbers rent asunder;
Friends forgot friends, foes fled to foes;—
And still the water rose and rose.

"Ah woe is me! Whom I have seen
Are now as though they had not been.
In the earth there is room for birth,
And there are graves enough in earth;
Why should the cold sea, tempest-torn,
Bury those whom it hath not borne?"
He answered not, and they went on.
The glory of the heavens was gone;
The moon gleamed not nor any star;
Cold winds were rustling near and far,
And from the trees the dry leaves fell,
With a sad sound unspeakable.
The air was cold; till from the South
A gust blew hot, like sudden drouth,
Into their faces; and a light,
Glowing and red, shone thro' the night.

A mighty city full of flame
And death and sounds without a name.

Amid the black and blinding smoke,
The people, as one man, awoke.
Oh! happy they who yesterday
On the long journey went away;
Whose pallid lips, smiling and chill,
While the flames scorch them smile on still;
Who murmur not; who tremble not
When the bier crackles fiery hot;
Who dying said in love's increase:
"Lord, let thy servant part in peace."

Those in the town could see and hear
A shaded river flowing near;
The broad deep bed could hardly hold
Its plenteous waters calm and cold.
Was flame-wrapt all the city wall,
The city gates were flame-wrapt all.
What was man's strength, what puissance then?
Women were mighty as strong men.
Some knelt in prayer, believing still,
Resigned unto a righteous will,
Bowing beneath the chastening rod,
Lost to the world, but found of God.
Some prayed for friend, for child, for wife;
Some prayed for faith; some prayed for life;
While some, proud even in death, hope gone,
Steadfast and still, stood looking on.

"Death—death—oh! let us fly from death;
Where'er we go it followeth;
All these are dead; and we alone
Remain to weep for what is gone.

What is this thing? thus hurriedly
To pass into eternity;
To leave the earth so full of mirth;
To lose the profit of our birth;
To die and be no more; to cease,
Having numbness that is not peace.
Let us go hence; and, even if thus
Death everywhere must go with us,
Let us not see the change, but see
Those who have been or still shall be."

He sighed, and they went on together;
Beneath their feet did the grass wither;
Across the heaven high overhead
Dark misty clouds floated and fled;
And in their bosom was the thunder,
And angry lightnings flashed out under,
Forked and red and menacing;
Far off the wind was muttering;
It seemed to tell, not understood,
Strange secrets to the listening wood.

Upon its wings it bore the scent
Of blood of a great armament:
Then saw they how on either side
Fields were down-trodden far and wide.
That morning at the break of day
Two nations had gone forth to slay.

As a man soweth so he reaps.
The field was full of bleeding heaps;
Ghastly corpses of men and horses
That met death at a thousand sources;

Repining

Cold limbs and putrefying flesh;
Long love-locks clotted to a mesh
That stifled; stiffened mouths beneath
Staring eyes that had looked on death.

But these were dead: these felt no more
The anguish of the wounds they bore.
Behold, they shall not sigh again,
Nor justly fear, nor hope in vain.
What if none wept above them?—is
The sleeper less at rest for this?
Is not the young child's slumber sweet
When no man watcheth over it?

These had deep calm; but all around
There was a deadly smothered sound,
The choking cry of agony
From wounded men who could not die;
Who watched the black wing of the raven
Rise like a cloud 'twixt them and heaven,
And in the distance flying fast
Beheld the eagle come at last.

She knelt down in her agony:
"O Lord, it is enough," said she:
"My heart's prayer putteth me to shame;
Let me return to whence I came.
Thou who for love's sake didst reprove,
Forgive me for the sake of love."

DREAMLAND

WHERE sunless rivers weep
  Their waves into the deep,
She sleeps a charmèd sleep;
  Awake her not.
Led by a single star,
She came from very far,
To seek where shadows are
  Her pleasant lot.

She left the rosy morn,
She left the fields of corn,
For twilight cold and lorn,
  And water springs.
Thro' sleep, as thro' a veil,
She sees the sky look pale,
And hears the nightingale
  That sadly sings.

Dream Land

Rest, rest, a perfect rest
Shed over brow and breast;
Her face is toward the west,
  The purple land.
She cannot see the grain
Ripening on hill and plain;
She cannot feel the rain
  Upon her hand.

Rest, rest, for evermore
Upon a mossy shore,
Rest, rest, that shall endure,
  Till time shall cease;—
Sleep that no pain shall wake,
Night that no morn shall break,
Till joy shall overtake
  Her perfect peace.

SHE SLEEPS A CHARMED SLEEP

WHILE roses are so red,
  While lilies are so white,
Shall a woman exalt her face
  Because it gives delight?
She 's not so sweet as a rose,
  A lily 's straighter than she,
And if she were as red or white
  She'd be but one of three.

Whether she flush in love's summer
  Or in its winter grow pale,
Whether she flaunt her beauty
  Or hide it away in a veil,
Be she red or white,
  And stand she erect or bowed,
Time will win the race he runs with her
  And hide her away in a shroud.

THE hope I dreamed of was a dream,
  Was but a dream; and now I wake,
Exceeding comfortless, and worn, and old,
  For a dream's sake.

I hang my harp upon a tree,
  A weeping willow in a lake;
I hang my silenced harp there, wrung and snapt
  For a dream's sake.

Lie still, lie still, my breaking heart;
  My silent heart, lie still and break:
Life, and the world, and mine own self, are changed
  For a dream's sake.

TWILIGHT CALM

OH pleasant eventide!
  Clouds on the western side
Grow gray and grayer hiding the warm sun:
The bees and birds, their happy labours done,
  Seek their close nests and bide.

  Screened in the leafy wood
  The stock-doves sit and brood:
The very squirrel leaps from bough to bough
But lazily; pauses; and settles now
  Where once he stored his food.

  One by one the flowers close,
  Lily and dewy rose
Shutting their tender petals from the moon:
The grasshoppers are still; but not so soon
  Are still the noisy crows.

BUT·NOT·SO·SOON·
ARE STILL THE
NOISY·CROWS·

The dormouse squats and eats
Choice little dainty bits
Beneath the spreading roots of a broad lime;
Nibbling his fill he stops from time to time
And listens where he sits.

From far the lowings come
Of cattle driven home:
From farther still the wind brings fitfully
The vast continual murmur of the sea,
Now loud, now almost dumb.

The gnats whirl in the air,
The evening gnats; and there
The owl opes broad his eyes and wings to sail
For prey; the bat wakes; and the shell-less snail
Comes forth clammy and bare.

Hark! that's the nightingale,
Telling the self-same tale
Her song told when this ancient earth was young:
So echoes answered when her song was sung
In the first wooded vale.

We call it love and pain,
The passion of her strain;
And yet we little understand or know.
Why should it not be rather joy that so
Throbs in each throbbing vein?

In separate herds the deer
Lie; here the bucks, and here
The does, and by its mother sleeps the fawn:
Through all the hours of night until the dawn
They sleep, forgetting fear.

Twilight Calm

The hare sleeps where it lies,
With wary half-closed eyes;
The cock has ceased to crow, the hen to cluck:
Only the fox is out, some heedless duck
Or chicken to surprise.

Remote, each single star
Comes out, till there they are
All shining brightly. How the dews fall damp!
While close at hand the glow-worm lights her lamp,
Or twinkles from afar.

But evening now is done
As much as if the sun
Day-giving had arisen in the East:
For night has come; and the great calm has ceased,
The quiet sands have run.

HOW comes it, Flora, that, whenever we
Play cards together, you invariably,
However the pack parts,
Still hold the Queen of Hearts?

I 've scanned you with a scrutinizing gaze,
Resolved to fathom these your secret ways:
But, sift them as I will,
Your ways are secret still.

I cut and shuffle; shuffle, cut, again;
But all my cutting, shuffling, proves in vain:
Vain hope, vain forethought too;
That Queen still falls to you.

I dropped her once, prepense; but, ere the deal
Was dealt, your instinct seemed her loss to feel:
"There should be one card more,"
You said, and searched the floor.

I cheated once; I made a private notch
In Heart-Queen's back, and kept a lynx-eyed watch;
Yet such another back
Deceived me in the pack:

The Queen of Clubs assumed by arts unknown
An imitative dint that seemed my own;
This notch, not of my doing,
Misled me to my ruin.

It baffles me to puzzle out the clue,
Which must be skill, or craft, or luck in you:
Unless, indeed, it be
Natural affinity.

"There should be one card more," you said

The Queen of Hearts.

JESSIE, Jessie Cameron,
  Hear me but this once," quoth he.
"Good luck go with you, neighbour's son,
  But I 'm no mate for you," quoth she.
Day was verging toward the night
  There beside the moaning sea,
Dimness overtook the light
  There where the breakers be.
"O Jessie, Jessie Cameron,
  I have loved you long and true."—
"Good luck go with you, neighbour's son,
  But I 'm no mate for you."

She was a careless, fearless girl,
  And made her answer plain,
Outspoken she to earl or churl,
  Kindhearted in the main,

But somewhat heedless with her tongue
  And apt at causing pain;
A mirthful maiden she and young,
  Most fair for bliss or bane.
"Oh long ago I told you so,
  I tell you so to-day:
Go you your way, and let me go
  Just my own free way."

The sea swept in with moan and foam,
  Quickening the stretch of sand;
They stood almost in sight of home;
  He strove to take her hand.
"Oh, can't you take your answer then,
  And won't you understand?
For me you 're not the man of men,
  I 've other plans are planned.
You 're good for Madge, or good for Cis,
  Or good for Kate, may be:
But what 's to me the good of this
  While you 're not good for me?"

They stood together on the beach,
  They two alone,
And louder waxed his urgent speech,
  His patience almost gone:
"Oh say but one kind word to me,
  Jessie, Jessie Cameron."—
"I 'd be too proud to beg," quoth she,
  And pride was in her tone.

And pride was in her lifted head,
  And in her angry eye,
And in her foot, which might have fled
  But would not fly.

Some say that he had gipsy blood,
  That in his heart was guile:
Yet he had gone through fire and flood
  Only to win her smile.
Some say his grandam was a witch,
  A black witch from beyond the Nile,
Who kept an image in a niche
  And talked with it the while.
And by her hut far down the lane
  Some say they would not pass at night,
Lest they should hear an unked strain
  Or see an unked sight.

Alas for Jessie Cameron!—
  The sea crept moaning, moaning nigher:
She should have hastened to begone,—
  The sea swept higher, breaking by her:
She should have hastened to her home
  While yet the west was flushed with fire,
But now her feet are in the foam,
  The sea-foam sweeping higher.
O mother, linger at your door,
  And light your lamp to make it plain;
But Jessie she comes home no more,
  No more again.

They stood together on the strand,
  They only each by each;
Home, her home, was close at hand,
  Utterly out of reach.
Her mother in the chimney nook
  Heard a startled sea-gull screech,
But never turned her head to look
  Towards the darkening beach:
Neighbours here and neighbours there
  Heard one scream, as if a bird
Shrilly screaming cleft the air:—
  That was all they heard.

Jessie she comes home no more,
  Comes home never;
Her lover's step sounds at his door
  No more for ever.
And boats may search upon the sea
  And search along the river,
But none know where the bodies be;
  Sea-winds that shiver,
Sea-birds that breast the blast,
  Sea-waves swelling,
Keep the secret first and last
  Of their dwelling.

Whether the tide so hemmed them round
  With its pitiless flow
That when they would have gone they found
  No way to go;
Whether she scorned him to the last
  With words flung to and fro,

Or clung to him when hope was past,
  None will ever know:
Whether he helped or hindered her,
  Threw up his life or lost it well,
The troubled sea for all its stir
  Finds no voice to tell.

Only watchers by the dying
  Have thought they heard one pray
Wordless, urgent; and replying
  One seem to say him nay:
And watchers by the dead have heard
  A windy swell from miles away,
With sobs and screams, but not a word
  Distinct for them to say:
And watchers out at sea have caught
  Glimpse of a pale gleam here or there,
Come and gone as quick as thought,
  Which might be hand or hair.

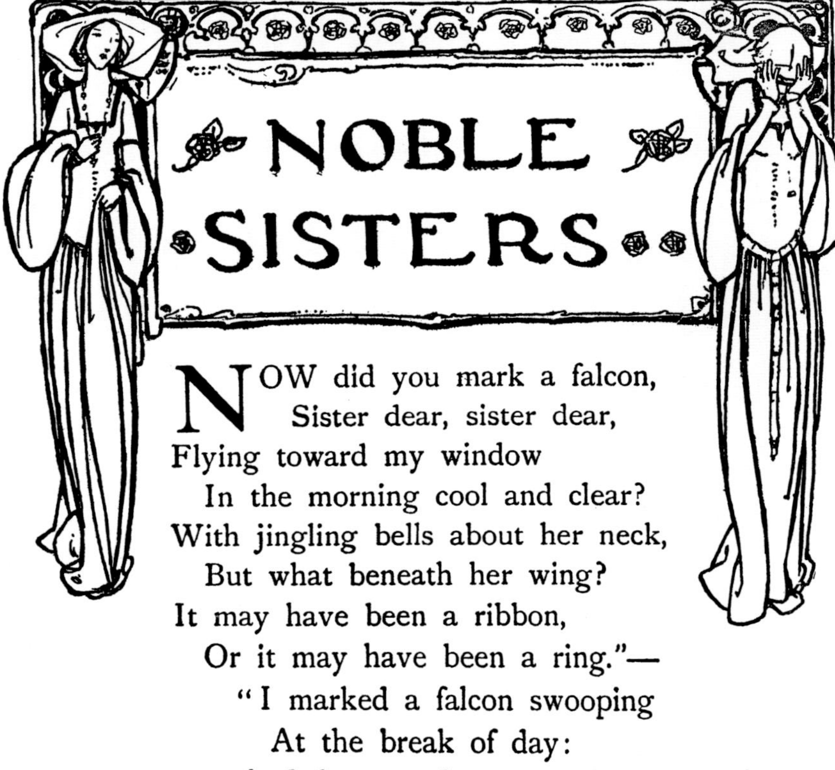

NOBLE SISTERS

NOW did you mark a falcon,
Sister dear, sister dear,
Flying toward my window
In the morning cool and clear?
With jingling bells about her neck,
But what beneath her wing?
It may have been a ribbon,
Or it may have been a ring."—
"I marked a falcon swooping
At the break of day:
And for your love, my sister dove
I frayed the thief away."—

"Or did you spy a ruddy hound,
Sister fair and tall,
Went snuffing round my garden bound,
Or crouched by my bower wall?

AND FOR YOUR LOVE MY SISTER DOVE
I FRAYED THE THIEF AWAY

With a silken leash about his neck;
  But in his mouth may be
A chain of gold and silver links,
  Or a letter writ to me."—
    "I heard a hound, highborn sister,
      Stood baying at the moon:
    I rose and drove him from your wall
      Lest you should wake too soon."—

"Or did you meet a pretty page
  Sat swinging on the gate;
Sat whistling whistling like a bird,
  Or may be slept too late:
With eaglets broidered on his cap,
  And eaglets on his glove?
If you had turned his pockets out,
  You had found some pledge of love."—
    "I met him at this daybreak,
      Scarce the east was red:
    Lest the creaking gate should anger you,
      I packed him home to bed."—

"Oh patience, sister. Did you see
  A young man tall and strong,
Swift-footed to uphold the right
  And to uproot the wrong,
Come home across the desolate sea
  To woo me for his wife?
And in his heart my heart is locked,
  And in his life my life."—
    "I met a nameless man, sister,
      Hard by your chamber door:

I said: 'Her husband loves her much,
And yet she loves him more'."—

"Fie, sister, fie, a wicked lie,
A lie, a wicked lie,
I have none other love but him,
Nor will have till I die.
And you have turned him from our door,
And stabbed him with a lie:
I will go seek him thro' the world
In sorrow till I die."—
"Go seek in sorrow, sister,
And find in sorrow too:
If thus you shame our father's name
My curse go forth with you."

UP-HILL

DOES the road wind up-hill all the way?
  Yes, to the very end.
Will the day's journey take the whole long day?
  From morn to night, my friend.

But is there for the night a resting-place?
  A roof for when the slow dark hours begin.
May not the darkness hide it from my face?
  You cannot miss that inn.

Shall I meet other wayfarers at night?
  Those who have gone before.
Then must I knock, or call when just in sight?
  They will not keep you standing at that door.

Shall I find comfort, travel-sore and weak?
  Of labour you shall find the sum.
Will there be beds for me and all who seek?
  Yea, beds for all who come.

THERE 'S blood between us, love, my love,
There 's father's blood, there 's brother's blood;
And blood 's a bar I cannot pass:
I choose the stairs that mount above,
Stair after golden skyward stair,
To city and to sea of glass.

My lily feet are soiled with mud,
With scarlet mud which tells a tale
Of hope that was, of guilt that was,
Of love that shall not yet avail;
Alas, my heart, if I could bare
My heart, this self-same stain is there:
I seek the sea of glass and fire
To wash the spot, to burn the snare;
Lo, stairs are meant to lift us higher:
Mount with me, mount the kindled stair.

THROUGH·THE·DARK·MY·
SILENCE·SPOKE·LIKE·
THUNDER·

Your eyes look earthward, mine look up.
I see the far-off city grand,
Beyond the hills a watered land,
Beyond the gulf a gleaming strand
Of mansions where the righteous sup;
Who sleep at ease among their trees,
Or wake to sing a cadenced hymn
With Cherubim and Seraphim;
They bore the Cross, they drained the cup,
Racked, roasted, crushed, wrenched limb from limb,
They the offscouring of the world:
The heaven of starry heavens unfurled,
The sun before their face is dim.

You looking earthward, what see you?
Milk-white, wine-flushed among the vines,
Up and down leaping, to and fro,
Most glad, most full, made strong with wines,
Blooming as peaches pearled with dew,
Their golden windy hair afloat,
Love-music warbling in their throat,
Young men and women come and go.

You linger, yet the time is short:
Flee for your life, gird up your strength
To flee; the shadows stretched at length
Show that day wanes, that night draws nigh;
Flee to the mountain, tarry not.
Is this a time for smile and sigh,
For songs among the secret trees
Where sudden blue birds nest and sport?
The time is short and yet you stay:

To-day, while it is called to-day,
Kneel, wrestle, knock, do violence, pray;
To-day is short, to-morrow nigh:
Why will you die? why will you die?

You sinned with me a pleasant sin:
Repent with me, for I repent,
Woe's me the lore I must unlearn!
Woe's me that easy way we went,
So rugged when I would return!
How long until my sleep begin,
How long shall stretch these nights and days?
Surely, clean Angels cry, she prays;
She laves her soul with tedious tears:
How long must stretch these years and years?

I turn from you my cheeks and eyes,
My hair which you shall see no more—
Alas for joy that went before,
For joy that dies, for love that dies!
Only my lips still turn to you,
My livid lips that cry, Repent.
O weary life, O weary Lent,
O weary time whose stars are few.

How should I rest in Paradise,
Or sit on steps of Heaven alone?
If Saints and Angels spoke of love,
Should I not answer from my throne:
Have pity upon me, ye my friends,
For I have heard the sound thereof:
Should I not turn with yearning eyes,
Turn earthwards with a pitiful pang?

Oh save me from a pang in Heaven.
By all the gifts we took and gave,
Repent, repent, and be forgiven:
This life is long, but yet it ends;
Repent and purge your soul and save:
No gladder song the morning stars
Upon their birthday morning sang
Than Angels sing when one repents.

I tell you what I dreamed last night;
A spirit with transfigured face
Fire-footed clomb an infinite space.
I heard his hundred pinions clang,
Heaven-bells rejoicing rang and rang,
Heaven-air was thrilled with subtle scents,
Worlds spun upon their rushing cars:
He mounted shrieking "Give me light";
Still light was pour'd on him, more light;
Angels, Archangels he outstripped,
Exultant in exceeding might,
And trod the skirts of Cherubim.
Still "Give me light", he shrieked; and dipped
His thirsty face, and drank a sea,
Athirst with thirst it could not slake.
I saw him, drunk with knowledge, take
From aching brows the aureole crown—
His locks writhed like a cloven snake—
He left his throne to grovel down
And lick the dust of Seraphs' feet:
For what is knowledge duly weighed?
Knowledge is strong, but love is sweet;
Yea all the progress he had made

Was but to learn that all is small
Save love, for love is all in all.

I tell you what I dreamed last night:
It was not dark, it was not light,
Cold dews had drenched my plenteous hair
Through clay; you came to seek me there.
And "Do you dream of me?" you said.
My heart was dust that used to leap
To you; I answered half asleep:
"My pillow is damp, my sheets are red,
There's a leaden tester to my bed:
Find you a warmer playfellow,
A warmer pillow for your head,
A kinder love to love than mine."
You wrung your hands: while I like lead,
Crushed downwards through the sodden earth:
You smote your hands but not in mirth,
And reeled but were not drunk with wine.

For all night long I dreamed of you:
I woke and prayed against my will,
Then slept to dream of you again.
At length I rose and knelt and prayed:
I cannot write the words I said,
My words were slow, my tears were few;
But through the dark my silence spoke
Like thunder. When this morning broke,
My face was pinched, my hair was gray,
And frozen blood was on the sill
Where stifling in my struggle I lay.

If now you saw me you would say:
Where is the face I used to love?
And I would answer: Gone before;
It tarries veiled in Paradise.
When once the morning star shall rise,
When earth with shadow flees away
And we stand safe within the door,
Then you shall lift the veil thereof.
Look up, rise up: for far above
Our palms are grown, our place is set;
There we shall meet as once we met,
And love with old familiar love.

STRIKE the bells wantonly,
Tinkle tinkle well;
Bring me wine, bring me flowers,
Ring the silver bell.
All my lamps burn scented oil,
Hung on laden orange-trees,
Whose shadowed foliage is the foil
To golden lamps and oranges.
Heap my golden plates with fruit,
Golden fruit, fresh-plucked and ripe;
Strike the bells and breathe the pipe;
Shut out showers from summer hours—
Silence that complaining lute—
Shut out thinking, shut out pain,
From hours that cannot come again.

Strike the bells solemnly,
Ding dong deep:
My friend is passing to his bed,
Fast asleep;

Strike the bells wantonly

A Peal of Bells.

There 's plaited linen round his head,
  While foremost go his feet—
His feet that cannot carry him.
My feast 's a show, my lights are dim;
  Be still, your music is not sweet,—
There is no music more for him:
  His lights are out, his feast is done:
His bowl that sparkled to the brim
Is drained, is broken, cannot hold;
My blood is chill; his blood is cold;
  His death is full, and mine begun.

SONG

OH roses for the flush of youth,
  And laurel for the perfect prime;
But pluck an ivy branch for me
  Grown old before my time.

Oh violets for the grave of youth,
  And bay for those dead in their prime;
Give me the withered leaves I chose
  Before in the old time.

GIVE·ME·THE·WITHERED·LEAVES·I·CHOSE BEFORE·IN·THE·OLD·TIME·

Love, strong as Death, is dead

An End.

LOVE, strong as Death, is dead.
Come, let us make his bed
Among the dying flowers:
A green turf at his head;
And a stone at his feet,
Whereon we may sit
In the quiet evening hours.

He was born in the Spring,
And died before the harvesting:
On the last warm summer day
He left us; he would not stay
For Autumn twilight cold and gray.
Sit we by his grave, and sing
He is gone away.

To few chords and sad and low
Sing we so:
Be our eyes fixed on the grass
Shadow-veiled as the years pass,
While we think of all that was
In the long ago.

REMEMBER me when I am gone away,
Gone far away into the silent land;
When you can no more hold me by the hand,
Nor I half turn to go yet turning stay.
Remember me when no more day by day
You tell me of our future that you planned:
Only remember me; you understand
It will be late to counsel then or pray.
Yet if you should forget me for a while
And afterwards remember, do not grieve:
For if the darkness and corruption leave
A vestige of the thoughts that once I had,
Better by far you should forget and smile
Than that you should remember and be sad.

Better by far you should forget and smile

Remember.

SONGS IN A CORNFIELD

A SONG in a cornfield
  Where corn begins to fall,
Where reapers are reaping,
  Reaping one, reaping all.
Sing pretty Lettice,
  Sing Rachel, sing May;
Only Marian cannot sing
  While her sweetheart 's away.

Where is he gone to
  And why does he stay?
He came across the green sea
  But for a day,
Across the deep green sea
  To help with the hay.
His hair was curly yellow
  And his eyes were gray,

He laughed a merry laugh
  And said a sweet say.
Where is he gone to
  That he comes not home?
To-day or to-morrow
  He surely will come.
Let him haste to joy
  Lest he lag for sorrow,
For one weeps to-day
  Who'll not weep to-morrow:
To-day she must weep
  For gnawing sorrow,
To-night she may sleep
  And not wake to-morrow.

May sang with Rachel
  In the waxing warm weather,
Lettice sang with them,
  They sang all together:—

"Take the wheat in your arm
  Whilst day is broad above,
Take the wheat to your bosom,
  But not a false false love.
  Out in the fields
    Summer heat gloweth,
  Out in the fields
    Summer wind bloweth,
  Out in the fields
    Summer friend showeth,
  Out in the fields
    Summer wheat groweth:

AND·SUM-
MER·FRIEND
·HAS·FLED·

But in the winter
  When summer heat is dead
And summer wind has veered
  And summer friend has fled,
Only summer wheat remaineth,
  White cakes and bread.
Take the wheat, clasp the wheat
  That 's food for maid and dove;
Take the wheat to your bosom,
  But not a false false love."

A silence of full noontide heat
  Grew on them at their toil:
The farmer's dog woke up from sleep.
  The green snake hid her coil.
Where grass stood thickest, bird and beast
  Sought shadows as they could,
The reaping men and women paused
  And sat down where they stood;
They ate and drank and were refreshed,
  For rest from toil is good

While the reapers took their ease,
  Their sickles lying by,
Rachel sang a second strain,
  And singing seemed to sigh:—

  "There goes the swallow—
Could we but follow!
  Hasty swallow stay,
  Point us out the way;
Look back swallow, turn back swallow, stop swallow.

"There went the swallow—
Too late to follow:
Lost our note of way,
Lost our chance to-day;
Good-bye swallow, sunny swallow, wise swallow.

"After the swallow
All sweet things follow;
All things go their way,
Only we must stay,
Must not follow; good-bye swallow, good swallow."

Then listless Marian raised her head
Among the nodding sheaves;
Her voice was sweeter than that voice·
She sang like one who grieves:
Her voice was sweeter than its wont
Among the nodding sheaves;
All wondered while they heard her sing
Like one who hopes and grieves:—

"Deeper than the hail can smite,
Deeper than the frost can bite,
Deep asleep through day and night,
Our delight.

"Now thy sleep no pang can break,
No to-morrow bid thee wake,
Not our sobs who sit and ache
For thy sake.

"Is it dark or light below?
Oh, but is it cold like snow?
Dost thou feel the green things grow
    Fast or slow?

"Is it warm or cold beneath,
Oh, but is it cold like death?
Cold like death, without a breath,
    Cold like death?"

If he comes to-day
  He will find her weeping;
If he comes to-morrow
  He will find her sleeping;
If he comes the next day
  He'll not find her at all,
He may tear his curling hair,
  Beat his breast and call.

THE GHOST'S PETITION

"THERE'S a footstep coming: look out, and see."—
 "The leaves are falling, the wind is calling;
No one cometh across the lea."—

"There's a footstep coming: O sister, look."—
 "The ripple flashes, the white foam dashes;
No one cometh across the brook."—

"But he promised that he would come:
 To-night, to-morrow, in joy or sorrow,
He must keep his word, and must come home.

"For he promised that he would come:
 His word was given; from earth or heaven,
He must keep his word, and must come home.

"Go to sleep, my sweet sister Jane;
 You can slumber, who need not number
Hour after hour in doubt and pain.

In the room centre stood her husband

The Ghost's Petition.

"I shall sit here awhile, and watch;
  Listening, hoping, for one hand groping
In deep shadow to find the latch."

After the dark, and before the light,
  One lay sleeping; and one sat weeping,
Who had watched and wept the weary night.

After the night, and before the day,
  One lay sleeping; and one sat weeping—
Watching, weeping for one away.

There came a footstep climbing the stair;
  Someone standing out on the landing
Shook the door like a puff of air—

Shook the door, and in he passed.
  Did he enter? In the room centre
Stood her husband: the door shut fast

"O Robin, but you are cold—
  Chilled with night-dew: so lily-white you
Look like a stray lamb from our fold.

"O Robin, but you are late:
  Come and sit near me—sit here and cheer me."—
(Blue the flame burnt in the grate.)

"Lay not down your head on my breast:
  I cannot hold you, kind wife, nor fold you
In the shelter that you love best.

"Feel not after my clasping hand:
  I am but a shadow, come from the meadow
Where many lie, but no tree can stand.

"We are trees which have shed their leaves:
  Our heads lie low there, but no tears flow there;
Only I grieve for my wife who grieves.

"I could rest if you would not moan
  Hour after hour; I have no power
To shut my ears where I lie alone.

"I could rest if you would not cry;
  But there 's no sleeping while you sit weeping—
Watching, weeping so bitterly."—

"Woe 's me! woe 's me! for this I have heard.
  Oh, night of sorrow!—oh, black to-morrow!
Is it thus that you keep your word?

"O you who used so to shelter me
  Warm from the least wind—why, now the east wind
Is warmer than you, whom I quake to see.

"O my husband of flesh and blood,
  For whom my mother I left, and brother,
And all I had, accounting it good,

"What do you do there, underground,
  In the dark hollow? I 'm fain to follow.
What do you do there?—what have you found?"—

"What I do there I must not tell:
  But I have plenty: kind wife, content ye:
It is well with us—it is well.

"Tender hand hath made our nest,
  Our fear is ended, our hope is blended
With present pleasure, and we have rest."—

"Oh, but Robin, I 'm fain to come,
  If your present days are so pleasant;
For my days are so wearisome.

"Yet I 'll dry my tears for your sake:
  Why should I tease you, who cannot please you
Any more with the pains I take?"

THE WORLD

BY day she woos me, soft, exceeding fair:
  But all night as the moon so changeth she;
  Loathsome and foul with hideous leprosy
And subtle serpents gliding in her hair.
By day she woos me to the outer air,
  Ripe fruits, sweet flowers, and full satiety:
  But thro' the night a beast she grins at me,
A very monster void of love and prayer.
By day she stands a lie: by night she stands
  In all the naked horror of the truth,
With pushing horns and clawed and clutching hands.
Is this a friend indeed; that I should sell
  My soul to her, give her my life and youth,
Till my feet, cloven too, take hold on hell?

All night as the moon so changeth she

The World.

EVERY valley drinks,
  Every dell and hollow:
Where the kind rain sinks and sinks,
  Green of Spring will follow.

Yet a lapse of weeks
  Buds will burst their edges,
Strip their wool-coats, glue-coats, streaks,
  In the woods and hedges;

Weave a bower of love
  For birds to meet each other,
Weave a canopy above
  Nest and egg and mother.

But for fattening rain
  We should have no flowers,
Never a bud or leaf again
  But for soaking showers;

Winter Rain

Never a mated bird
  In the rocking tree-tops,
Never indeed a flock or herd
  To graze upon the lea-crops.

Lambs so woolly white,
  Sheep the sun-bright leas on,
They could have no grass to bite
  But for rain in season.

We should find no moss
  In the shadiest places,
Find no waving meadow grass
  Pied with broad-eyed daisies:

But miles of barren sand,
  With never a son or daughter;
Not a lily on the land,
  Or lily on the water.

CROAK, croak, croak,"
Thus the Raven spoke,
Perched on his crooked tree,
As black as black could be.
Shun him and fear him,
Lest the Bridegroom hear him;
Scout him and rout him
With his ominous eye about him.

Yet, "Croak, croak, croak,"
Still tolled from the oak,
From that fatal black bird,
Whether heard or unheard:
"O ship upon the high seas,
Freighted with lives and spices,
Sink, O ship," croaked the Raven:
"Let the Bride mount to heaven."

In a far foreign land
Upon the wave-edged sand,
Some friends gaze wistfully
Across the glittering sea.
"If we could clasp our sister,"
Three say: "now we have missed her!"
"If we could kiss our daughter!"
Two sigh across the water.

Oh, the ship sails fast
With silken flags at the mast,
And the home-wind blows soft;
But a Raven sits aloft,
Chuckling and choking,
Croaking, croaking, croaking:—
Let the Bridegroom keep watch keenly
For this choice Bride mild and queenly

On a sloped sandy beach,
Which the springtide billows reach,
Stand a watchful throng
Who have hoped and waited long:
"Fie on this ship that tarries
With the priceless freight it carries.
The time seems long and longer:
O languid wind, wax stronger;"—

Whilst the Raven perched at ease
Still croaks and does not cease,
One monotonous note
Tolled from his iron throat:
"No father, no mother,
But I have a sable brother:

He sees where ocean flows to,
And he knows what he knows too."

A day and a night
They kept watch worn and white;
A night and a day
For the swift ship on its way:
For the Bride and her maidens—
Clear chimes the bridal cadence—
For the tall ship that never
Hove in sight for ever.

On either shore, some
Stand in grief loud or dumb
As the dreadful dread
Grows certain tho' unsaid.
For laughter there is weeping,
And waking instead of sleeping,
And a desperate sorrow
Morrow after morrow.

Oh who knows the truth?
How she perished in her youth,
And like a queen went down
Pale in her royal crown:
How she went up to glory
From the sea-foam chill and hoary,
An innocent queen and holy,
To a high throne from a lowly?

They went down, all the crew,
The silks and spices too,
The great ones and the small,
One and all, one and all.

A Bird's-eye View

Was it thro' stress of weather,
Quicksands, rocks, or all together?
Only the Raven knows this,
And he will not disclose this.—

After a day and a year
The bridal bell chimes clear;
After a year and a day
The Bridegroom is brave and gay.
Love is sound, faith is rotten;
The old Bride is forgotten:—
Two ominous Ravens only
Remember, black and lonely.

YOUNG Love lies sleeping
  In May time of the year,
Among the lilies,
  Lapped in the tender light:
White lambs come grazing,
  White doves come building there,
And round about him
  The May bushes are white.

Soft moss the pillow,
  For oh! a softer cheek;
Broad leaves cast shadow
  Upon the heavy eyes:
There winds and waters
  Grow lulled, and scarcely speak;
There twilight lingers
  The longest in the skies.

Young Love lies dreaming;
  But who shall tell the dream?—
A perfect sunlight
  On rustling forest tips;
Or perfect moonlight
  Upon a rippling stream;
Or perfect silence,
  Or song of cherished lips.

Burn odours round him
  To fill the drowsy air,
Weave silent dances
  Around him to and fro:
For oh! in waking
  The sights are not so fair,
And song and silence
  Are not like these below.

Young Love lies dreaming
  Till summer days are gone,
Dreaming and drowsing
  Away to perfect sleep:
He sees the beauty
  Sun hath not looked upon,
And tastes the fountain
  Unutterably deep.

Him perfect music
  Doth hush unto his rest,
And through the pauses
  The perfect silence calms:

Young Love lies drowsing

Dream-love.

Oh! poor the voices
  Of earth from east to west,
And poor earth's stillness
  Between her stately palms.

Young Love lies drowsing
  Away to poppied death;
Cool shadows deepen
  Across the sleeping face:
So fails the summer
  With warm delicious breath,
And what hath autumn
  To give us in its place?

Draw close the curtains
  Of branched evergreen;
Change cannot touch them
  With fading fingers sere:
Here the first violets
  Perhaps will bud unseen,
And a dove, may be,
  Return to nestle here.

A·TESTIMONY

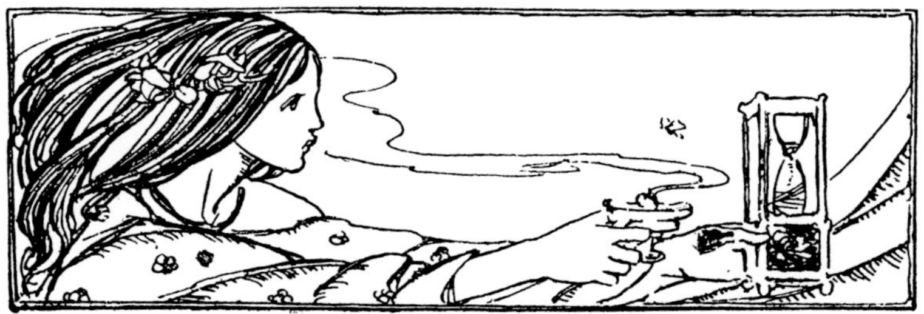

I SAID of laughter: it is vain.
  Of mirth I said: what profits it?
  Therefore I found a book, and writ
Therein how ease and also pain,
How health and sickness, every one
Is vanity beneath the sun.

Man walks in a vain shadow; he
  Disquieteth himself in vain.
  The things that were shall be again;
The rivers do not fill the sea,
But turn back to their secret source;
The winds too turn upon their course.

Our treasures moth and rust corrupt,
  Or thieves break through and steal, or they
  Make themselves wings and fly away.
One man made merry as he supped,
Nor guessed how when that night grew dim
His soul would be required of him.

We build our houses on the sand
  Comely withoutside and within;
  But when the winds and rains begin
To beat on them, they cannot stand:
They perish, quickly overthrown,
Loose from the very basement stone.

All things are vanity, I said:
  Yea vanity of vanities.
  The rich man dies; and the poor dies:
The worm feeds sweetly on the dead.
Whate'er thou lackest, keep this trust:
All in the end shall have but dust:

The one inheritance, which best
  And worst alike shall find and share:
  The wicked cease from troubling there,
And there the weary be at rest;
There all the wisdom of the wise
Is vanity of vanities.

Man flourishes as a green leaf,
  And as a leaf doth pass away;
  Or as a shade that cannot stay
And leaves no track, his course is brief:
Yet man doth hope and fear and plan
Till he is dead:—oh foolish man!

Our eyes cannot be satisfied
  With seeing, nor our ears be filled
  With hearing: yet we plant and build
And buy and make our borders wide;
We gather wealth, we gather care,
But know not who shall be our heir.

A Testimony

Why should we hasten to arise
  So early, and so late take rest?
  Our labour is not good; our best
Hopes fade; our heart is stayed on lies.
Verily, we sow wind; and we
Shall reap the whirlwind, verily.

He who hath little shall not lack;
  He who hath plenty shall decay:
  Our fathers went; we pass away;
Our children follow on our track:
So generations fail, and so
They are renewed and come and go.

The earth is fattened with our dead;
  She swallows more and doth not cease:
  Therefore her wine and oil increase
And her sheaves are not numberèd;
Therefore her plants are green, and all
Her pleasant trees lusty and tall.

Therefore the maidens cease to sing,
  And the young men are very sad;
  Therefore the sowing is not glad,
And mournful is the harvesting.
Of high and low, of great and small,
Vanity is the lot of all.

A King dwelt in Jerusalem;
  He was the wisest man on earth;
  He had all riches from his birth,
And pleasures till he tired of them;
Then, having tested all things, he
Witnessed that all are vanity.

VANITY · OF · VANITIES .

WINTER is cold-hearted,
Spring is yea and nay,
Autumn is a weathercock
Blown every way:
Summer days for me
When every leaf is on its tree;

When Robin's not a beggar,
And Jenny Wren's a bride,
And larks hang singing, singing, singing,
Over the wheat-fields wide,
And anchored lilies ride,
And the pendulum spider
Swings from side to side,
And blue-black beetles transact business,
And gnats fly in a host,
And furry caterpillars hasten
That no time be lost,
And moths grow fat and thrive,
And ladybirds arrive.

Summer

Before green apples blush,
  Before green nuts embrown,
Why, one day in the country
  Is worth a month in town;
  Is worth a day and a year
Of the dusty, musty, lag-last fashion
  That days drone elsewhere.

WHERE were you last night? I watched at the gate;
I went down early, I stayed down late.
Were you snug at home, I should like to know,
Or were you in the coppice wheedling Kate?

She's a fine girl, with a fine clear skin;
Easy to woo, perhaps not hard to win.
Speak up like a man and tell me the truth:
I'm not one to grow downhearted and thin.

If you love her best, speak up like a man;
It's not I will stand in the light of your plan:
Some girls might cry and scold you a bit,
And say they couldn't bear it; but I can.

Love was pleasant enough, and the days went fast;
Pleasant while it lasted, but it needn't last;
Awhile on the wax, and awhile on the wane,
Now dropped away into the past.

Was it pleasant to you? To me it was:
Now clean gone as an image from glass,
  As a goodly rainbow that fades away,
As dew that steams upward from the grass,

As the first spring day or the last summer day,
As the sunset flush that leaves heaven grey,
  As a flame burnt out for lack of oil,
Which no pains relight or ever may.

Good luck to Kate and good luck to you:
I guess she'll be kind when you come to woo.
  I wish her a pretty face that will last,
I wish her a husband steady and true.

Hate you? not I, my very good friend;
All things begin and all have an end.
  But let broken be broken; I put no faith
In quacks who set up to patch and mend.

Just my love and one word to Kate—
Not to let time slip if she means to mate;
  For even such a thing has been known
As to miss the chance while we weigh and wait.

WHEN I was dead, my spirit turned
  To seek the much-frequented house:
I passed the door, and saw my friends
  Feasting beneath green orange boughs;
From hand to hand they pushed the wine,
  They sucked the pulp of plum and peach;
They sang, they jested, and they laughed,
  For each was loved of each.

I listened to their honest chat.
  Said one: "To-morrow we shall be
Plod plod along the featureless sands
  And coasting miles and miles of sea."
Said one: "Before the turn of tide
  We will achieve the eyrie-seat."
Said one: "To-morrow shall be like
  To-day, but much more sweet."

" To-morrow," said they, strong with hope,
  And dwelt upon the pleasant way:
" To-morrow," cried they one and all,
  While no one spoke of yesterday.
Their life stood full at blessed noon;
  I, only I, had passed away:
" To-morrow and to-day," they cried;
  I was of yesterday.

I shivered comfortless, but cast
  No chill across the tablecloth;
I all-forgotten shivered, sad
  To stay and yet to part how loth:
I passed from the familiar room,
  I who from love had passed away,
Like the remembrance of a guest
  That tarrieth but a day.

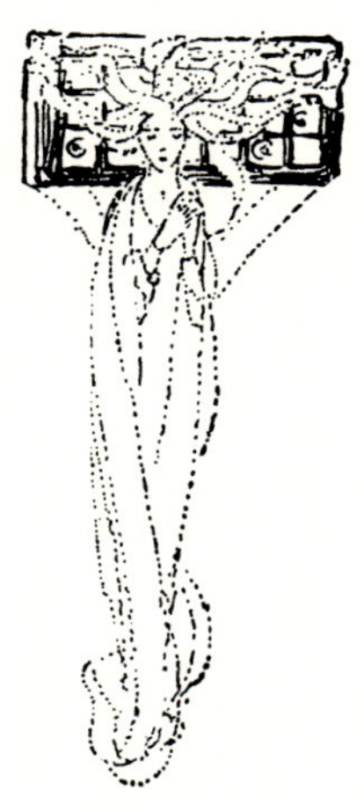

I passed from the familiar room

At Home.

I WILL tell you when they met:
In the limpid days of spring;
Elder boughs were budding yet,
Oaken boughs looked wintry still,
But primrose and veined violet
In the mossful turf were set,
While meeting birds made haste to sing
And build with right good will.

I will tell you when they parted:
When plenteous autumn sheaves were brown,
Then they parted heavy-hearted;
The full rejoicing sun looked down
As grand as in the days before;
Only they had lost a crown;
Only to them those days of yore
Could come back nevermore.

One Day

When shall they meet? I cannot tell,
Indeed, when they shall meet again,
Except some day in Paradise:
For this they wait, one waits in pain.
Beyond the sea of death love lies
For ever, yesterday, to-day;
Angels shall ask them, "Is it well?"
And they shall answer "Yea".

LIVE all thy sweet life thro',
  Sweet Rose, dew-sprent,
Drop down thine evening dew
To gather it anew
When day is bright:
  I fancy thou wast meant
Chiefly to give delight.

Sing in the silent sky,
  Glad soaring bird;
Sing out thy notes on high
To sunbeam straying by
Or passing cloud;
  Heedless if thou art heard
Sing thy full song aloud.

Oh that it were with me
  As with the flower;

Blooming on its own tree
For butterfly and bee
Its summer morns:
  That I might bloom mine hour
A rose in spite of thorns.

Oh that my work were done
  As birds' that soar
Rejoicing in the sun:
That when my time is run
And daylight too,
  I so might rest once more
Cool with refreshing dew.

CHILD'S·TALK·IN·APRIL

I WISH you were a pleasant wren,
  And I your small accepted mate;
How we 'd look down on toilsome men!
  We 'd rise and go to bed at eight
  Or it may be not quite so late.

Then you should see the nest I 'd build,
  The wondrous nest for you and me;
The outside rough perhaps, but filled
  With wool and down: ah, you should see
  The cosy nest that it would be.

We 'd have our change of hope and fear,
  Small quarrels, reconcilements sweet:
I 'd perch by you to chirp and cheer,
  Or hop about on active feet
  And fetch you dainty bits to eat.

We 'd be so happy by the day,
  So safe and happy through the night,
We both should feel, and I should say,
  It 's all one season of delight,
And we 'll make merry whilst we may.

Perhaps some day there 'd be an egg
  When spring had blossomed from the snow
I 'd stand triumphant on one leg;
  Like chanticleer I 'd almost crow
  To let our little neighbours know.

Next you should sit and I would sing
Through lengthening days of sunny spring:
  Till, if you wearied of the task,
I 'd sit; and you should spread your wing
  From bough to bough; I 'd sit and bask.

Fancy the breaking of the shell,
  The chirp, the chickens wet and bare,
The untried proud paternal swell;
  And you with housewife-matron air
  Enacting choicer bills of fare.

Fancy the embryo coats of down,
  The gradual feathers soft and sleek;
Till clothed and strong from tail to crown,
  With virgin warblings in their beak,
  They too go forth to soar and seek.

So would it last an April through
And early summer fresh with dew:
  Then should we part and live as twain,
Love-time would bring me back to you
  And build our happy nest again.

WHEN I am dead, my dearest,
  Sing no sad songs for me;
Plant thou no roses at my head,
  Nor shady cypress tree:
Be the green grass above me
  With showers and dewdrops wet;
And if thou wilt, remember,
  And if thou wilt, forget.

I shall not see the shadows,
  I shall not feel the rain;
I shall not hear the nightingale
  Sing on as if in pain:
And dreaming through the twilight
  That doth not rise nor set,
Haply I may remember,
  And haply may forget.

GOBLIN MARKET AND OTHER SELECTED POEMS

Printed and Bound in China by RR Donnelley.

Printed on 157 gsm Chinese matte art paper.
Bound in JHT cloth.

DISTRIBUTED BY DOVER PUBLICATIONS, INC.